THE
INFINITY
ROOM

THE INFINITY ROOM

POEMS BY GARY FINCKE

WHEELBARROW BOOKS ▪ *East Lansing*

⊗ The paper used in this publication meets the minimum requirements
of ANSI/NISO Z39.48-1992 (R 1997) (Permanence of Paper).

 Wheelbarrow Books
Michigan State University Press
East Lansing, Michigan 48823-5245

Printed and bound in the United States of America.

28 27 26 25 24 23 22 21 20 19   1 2 3 4 5 6 7 8 9 10

Library of Congress Control Number: 2018939765
ISBN 978-1-61186-310-9 (paper)
ISBN 978-1-60917-589-4 (PDF)
ISBN 978-1-62895-353-4 (ePub)
ISBN 978-1-62896-353-3 (Kindle)

Book design by Charlie Sharp, Sharp Des!gns, East Lansing, MI
Cover design by Shaun Allshouse, www.shaunallshouse.com
Cover art is "Atom bomb mushroom cloud made of ash," by domagoj8888,
and is used under license from Adobe Stock.

G green
  press
  INITIATIVE Michigan State University Press is a member of the Green Press
Initiative and is committed to developing and encouraging
ecologically responsible publishing practices. For more information about the
Green Press Initiative and the use of recycled paper in book publishing, please
visit *www.greenpressinitiative.org.*

Visit Michigan State University Press at *www.msupress.org*

For Derek, Shannon, Aaron,
and, as always, Liz

With the publication of Gary Fincke's *The Infinity Room*, the Residential College in the Arts and Humanities (RCAH) Center for Poetry at Michigan State University offers our third book in a long-dreamed-of project, the Wheelbarrow Books Poetry Series. Clearly, we pay homage to William Carlos Williams and his iconic poem, "The Red Wheelbarrow." Readers will remember the poem begins, "so much depends upon" that red wheelbarrow. We believe that in the early decades of this twenty-first century, a time when technology, politics, and globalization are changing our lives at a pace we could hardly have imagined, so much does depend upon our determination to privilege the voices of our poets, new and old, and to make those voices available to a wide audience. So much depends upon providing a retreat, a place of stillness and contemplation, a place of safety and inspiration. So much depends upon our ability to have access to the words of others so that we see, regardless of race, religion, ethnicity, gender, economic situation, or geographical location, that we all share the human condition, that we are more alike than we are different. Poetry helps us do that. The eighteenth-century British philosopher-statesman Edmund Burke argued that the highest form of the moral imagination was found in poetry and art. In pursuit of the well-ordered life, he believed writers and artists were our greatest help. Edward Hirsch reminds us that poetry is one solitude speaking to another—across time, across space, across all our differences. Audre Lorde reminds us that poetry is not a luxury; it is a necessity. Walt Whitman knew that to have great poets, we must create great audiences. As our number of published books increases, we hope that our audience will also increase. So much depends upon the collaboration of our readers and writers, the intimate ways these poems help them come to know one another.

—ANITA SKEEN, *Wheelbarrow Books Series Editor*

After reading the first couple of poems in this collection, "Distraction Therapy" and "The Perimeter Melody," I was so impressed that I anticipated the disappointment that comes from knowing that certain stunning performances cannot be maintained. I was mistaken. The quality persists. The poet takes the reader through his landscape, never losing the reader's attention. I am continually struck by images that rise with the delicacy of helium balloons, finally making contact with—at first—improbabilities (as do the Metaphysical Poets) that soon become not merely probable but as convincing as certainty and in ways that enlarge our perceptions.

The poet holds our hands, separating us from where we were in a way, leading us down the mine shaft of his vision, one in which we see perfectly, even as far as those remote layers of meaning. All this is done so richly, convincingly, that we forget our starting points, where we came from, with no special desire to return to the usual—whether morning coffee, a favorite concert, or a walk around a place of revelation—but instead maintain a driving curiosity to stay with the revelation in these poems, to explore further, because we realize that this poet's mission touches us in ways we cannot ignore.

I feel touched to have been given the honor of reading this manuscript before it acquired its covers.

—GEORGE ELLENBOGEN

Contents

1   Distraction Therapy

i.

5   The Perimeter Melody
6   For Good
7   During the Retirement Semester
9   The Earth, We're Told, Is Humming
11 The Malignancy of Stars
12 The Fury that Follows Small Disappointments
14 The Fear Warehouse
15 Shadowing the Gravedigger
17 Assessing the Dead
19 Science
21 The Shelter Revival
23 The Infinity Room
26 The Startling Language of Shriveling Leaves
28 Preserving Cursive
30 The Lost Continents
33 The Secret City

ii.

45 The Absolute
46 After the Bomb Drill, Miss Hartung Teaches Weather
47 The Nuclear Age
49 Upon the Tongue
50 While I Am Standing
52 The Light
56 The Rain after Sunrise
57 The Secret Voice

58   Stunned

59   A Blanket Was over Her Body

61   Merging, Slowing, the Second Sun

63   Worship

65   The Sum Total

67   The Lengthening Radius for Hate: A Sequence

iii.

89   The Chernobyl Swallows

90   Turning Sixty-Five: How to Rid Your House of Ghosts

93   Visiting the Living Writers Class

95   The Hands

97   Dreamtime

99   Elegy

104   Anniversary

107   ACKNOWLEDGMENTS

THE
INFINITY
ROOM

Distraction Therapy

To manage fear, start anywhere
and count backwards by threes and eights.
Or multiply—the times tables

can soothe the heart. To slow breathing,
tap your feet. Do knee bends. If you
hum melodies, you will believe

you're dancing. To stop panic,
try anagrams or spell the names
for where you are. Find all the words

within them. Keep track of your score.
To break anxiety, focus
on something far in front of you.

Walk toward it, totaling your steps.
To resist the next bad moment,
press one hand into the other.

To handle the next after that,
grip them tight and begin to pull.
The hands are antidotes. Pit left

against the right. Feel that? Each time
you fight yourself, you smother fear.
To keep from dying, remember

the times you've survived. That list holds
all the terrors you imagine.
Read them aloud. Then breathe. Then breathe.

i.

The Perimeter Melody

A thirty-kilometer radius exclusion zone
surrounds Chernobyl.

Silence is fingertips reading the alphabet.
The first word is *warning,* the second, *forbidden.*

Inside the zone, there is an inhabited house
From which the future will be clearly understood.

Laundry hovers on clotheslines like returning birds.
A woman examines the field where her neighbors

Are absent. When the wind rises, she imagines
The all-day music played for Chernobyl's guardsmen,

Their rooms, so close to hell, declared prone to madness.
Her sheets begin their stuttered song. A shirt whispers

Its verse of vacancy. If she walks two hundred
And twenty paces, she will reach the barbed wire where

Earth's edge has broken. Along its perimeter
Is the gorgeous border where bearable begins.

For Good

He's dead and gone, and yet you read
That a man in Serbia has
Driven a stake into the grave
Of Slobodan Milošević.
As if superstition has not
Been domesticated to flags
And flowers, as if you might walk
To the gravesites of those you hate
In order to spike the soil
And repeat, seven times, "For good."
As if you might haul that stake home
In the trunk of your car, something
To keep in the garage among
The garden tools, the grave's earth dried
And caked upon its brittle point.
As if, in March, you hammer it
Into the ground among a bed
Of perennials. As if, through
April, you examine the earth,
And when every bud reappears
You weep and bring that stake inside
Where there's a place beside your bed,
Your hand reaching for it each time
The darkness speaks its dialect
Of shame, holding its point over
Your heart to coerce a symbol,
The Milošević of yourself
As adamant as April while
You rehearse like a citizen
Of a tiny theocracy
Where consolation can be held
Like a stark, sacred affliction.

During the Retirement Semester

My students, in unison, say they are
veterans of school lockdowns, that we meet
in a room as exposed as a hostage.
They have friends abroad in Paris, ones who
ordered a safe, early dinner inside
the terrorists' selected restaurant.
When Marlena says she hopes her shooter
is a woman who believes in something,
the class agrees there is nothing stranger
than sacrificing a life for faith, and
because we are inside a rectory
refurbished for our workshops, or because
they're young, I say that a girl I once kissed
declared she was saving herself for . . . then
paused and looked away as if the object
of her soft preposition was close by,
that who she became was a former nun,
thirty years and leaving as if she'd been
waiting for retirement's full benefits,
that she laughed easily and lived alone
in a studio apartment she cramped
with wall-length shelves of holy replicas.
None of them remember seeing a nun,
even the two who were raised Catholic,
and they chatter about obsolescence,
cheery with distraction, barely younger
than the archivist who had asked me, just
before class, what audience I believed
had interest enough to examine
what I'd boxed and filed. Extraordinary,
she said, her voice emptying my office,
the door, off plumb, nearly closing itself

behind her as if, inside that former
bedroom of priests, privacy were powered
by some forgotten relic they'd once shown
to their housekeepers, aging nuns who lived
below them in half the space, their comfort
sacrificed for the artless needs of God.

The Earth, We're Told, Is Humming

Beneath our feet, we're told, the ground
is always moving. Plates that shift,
continental, oceanic,
the water above creating
chorus as it rises and falls
with the moon. That hum, moreover,
is sometimes audible, a low
murmur that keeps a few of us
awake. Torture, one woman says—
headaches, nosebleeds, insomnia
following the gifted like plagues.

Now somebody records this hum
and broadcasts it online from Maine.
Speeded and amplified, he claims,
the sound is what a fetus hears
in the womb, citing how children
sitting near his speakers curl in
on themselves, how adults weep through
humming nightmares, how this monster
under the bed is the bleak groan
of instability seeping
up like badly buried waste. But

now, this morning brings the story
of the spadefoot toad that burrows
deeply beneath the desert. That
half-sleeps for weeks or even months
while listening for the sound of
a raindrop on the sand above.
Sometimes years, it takes, for that drop
to multiply sufficiently

to prompt that toad to claw its way
to a downpour, sounding its song
of desire for other toads who
have heard the rain and risen. Now,

the toads will synchronize their calls,
communal voice necessity.
Alone and singing, those toads are
easy prey, but bunched in chorus
they are safe, not because of strength,
but because coyotes will not
attack a swarm and owls require
a single target, all those eyes
and ears alert for toads designed
to ravage them one at a time
when they emerge from this earth so
sensitive it transmits the time
to sing our songs of endurance.

The Malignancy of Stars

Two hours to any sort of daylight,
yet a neighbor watches his wall-width screen.
A garbage truck makes just two stops along
our cul-de-sac street; the paper boy creeps
in his chuffing car. Beyond my neighbor's,
an ambulance has been parked an hour
at the seniors complex where three friends live.
I figure the odds and drop to the floor
for the sit-ups and pushups that follow
coffee. Consider this, I tell myself.
And I settle upon the belief in
the malignancy of stars, how bodies
may be selected from a great distance
for diseases. My oral surgeon, just before
my last appointment, has been felled
by a cancer so rare his specialist
had never seen one. Yesterday, I learned
his practice is closed. The receptionist
promised to send my records once I sign
a waiver—x-rays before and after
surgery, additional ones to probe
serious complications. When I walk
to the newspaper, I am close enough
to make out what's on, a woman speaking
from a bare stage, her gestures emphatic
and earnest. The camera finds women
in the audience whose faces are rapt
with belief in whatever has been said.
And though the power of any star but
ours is as implausible as faith,
the morning whispers attrition, the squalls
of constellations pass patiently low.

The Fury that Follows Small Disappointments

One hundred and sixty copies
Of the *Harrisburg Patriot*
Have unraveled on the sidewalk.
Vandals. The wind. And it's too late
To help the carrier an hour
From his dawn delivery.
The pages lift and settle.
They tumble and catch on porches,
Shrubbery, trees, and from upstairs
I see the huge, white wings of them
Soaring in the cold front gusts.
I think of siding and shingles
I've collected from neighbors' yards,
Gathering my stripped possessions
While they inspected the fitness
Of their contractors' skills. I think
Of the fury that follows
Small disappointments: paragraphs
Of rant, punctuated by curse.
And for a moment the street seems
Out of breath. Open pages sink
To pavement and lawn. And I can
Imagine all of us stepping
Into the threatening morning
To gather thick sections and light,
Unfolded pages, bringing them
Into our houses to heal.
A car approaches, dragging
The rain behind it. After
It passes, the newspapers lurch
Upward and stumble, heavy
With water. There might be pages

Huddling among the cornstalks
Across the road, some of them caught
And repeating their stories
Before the storm soaks them mute.
When one insert unfurls close
To this window, it flutters
Like memory's beautiful
Reporting before descending,
Sincere, remarkable, unread.

The Fear Warehouse

Neurologists have learned where rats store their fear.

—News Item

Missionaries come to my door this morning,
Speaking through the screen about the end-times
That are running, one says, on fumes, grinning
Like the bright dot on my Celica's fuel gauge
When I am fifteen minutes from stalling.
Those preachers hope to stir the fear I've stored
Since a thousand Sunday sermons rooted it
So deeply I could imagine a soul.
They speak with the fervor of plague-year priests,
The certainty of bloodletters draining
The body to rebalance its humors,
The four I studied once, remembering
The barber, past seventy, who had cut
My schoolboy hair, how, a decade later,
He stood with me outside his long-closed shop
And recited the contours of my head,
The crown's showy cowlick he oiled down
While he revealed the blood and bandages
Of the barber pole to mannequin me.
The street was becoming a plain of absence
For an approaching thruway. My hair curled
Over my collar; the veins in my arms
Seemed suddenly swollen the way they feel
As I watch those two terrorists enter
The house of the woman across the street,
Admitted by the daughter who cuts herself
Daily, drawing a blade across her limbs
As if she were lancing the boils of fear,
Squandering herself on anticipation.

14

Shadowing the Gravedigger

Because I have asked him, I am
In the gravedigger's truck waiting
For a funeral to finish.
To show respect, I am wearing
My best topcoat to cover jeans.
There is a distance named discrete,
And he maintains it for his job.
He never plays the radio.

The gravedigger says there are times
He shovels by hand for infants
And the cremated, holes too small
For the spade of machinery.
For those, weather is important,
The earth, if frozen, is a bitch.

Below zero, it was, the day
My mother was buried, backhoe
Visible on a nearby rise,
Mound of earth covered by something
Designed to look like summer sod.
The pastor worked January
Into meaning, snow and zero
Entwined like the benevolent
Grasp of God until we performed
The chilled amen of erasure.

My sister, four hours from here,
Stores mementoes of our parents—
A pressed dark suit, a Sunday dress.
Alone in her house, I've opened
Her bedroom closet like a thief.

Just what does she anticipate?
To dress them for judgment the way
She prepared them for burial?
I have alibis for missing
Tenderness. Yes, I was elsewhere.

Once, I say, I watched as an urn
Was laid into a grave behind
A local church. The woman's one
Surviving son shoveled soil
While the minister recited
A prayer we could follow along
The page of a printed program.

The gravedigger watches the crowd
For the retreat to cars. He talks
Over the premonition that
Insists like a tinnitus shriek.
A child must be more difficult
Than a baby, I try, and he
Says he's opened and closed the earth
For his father; now his mother
Has entered hospice. I cannot
Fill in the silence. Whatever
You can bear, he says, and we do.

Assessing the Dead

When Gettysburg's dead, years buried,
were unearthed for removal
to national cemeteries,
someone was hired to separate
Union from Confederate.
Relying, at first, upon
jacket color, he made certain
the loyal were rewarded.

My sister, twice, has studied
photographs to perfect display,
learning which necklace our mother
wore with her blue, Sunday-only
lace-trimmed dress, how, exactly,
our father's awards were arranged
for ceremony when he put on
his scoutmaster's uniform,
placing those reframed portraits
alongside both coffins like
mirrors or proof of love.

For the difficult cases,
uniform color unknown,
the grave-shifter was taught
to recognize the brand names
of shoes and the quality
of underwear to mark bones
qualified for respected graves.

And now we've learned elephants
investigate the bones of their dead
by smell and touch, using the tips

of their trunks to caress what's left.
And yes, sometimes the young can
identify their parents,
lingering longer to inspect,
or, we like to imagine,
reflect. And whether saddened
or comforted by the ordeal
of recollection, they examine
the contours of the whitened skull.
Which is how reverie begins.
Then how it ends in turning away,
the necessary going on.

Science

Two wives this man throttled and, what's more,
Chopped them into pieces, fitting so much
The part of born-to-be-awful, a doctor,
After the execution, measured the skull,
The set of the eyes and the forehead's slope,
The jaw that seemed fixed by chronic rage.

As if there were postmortems for evil,
He floated the killer's brain in a jar.
Meaning, this morning, my wife and I,
In a museum so empty we can spend
As long as we want with his display,
Remember descriptions that begin
With "you'd never guess" or "he seemed so nice,"
What I'd said about the physics teacher,
Three rooms from mine, how neatly he wore
His coat, white shirt, and tie as we managed
The large-group discipline situation
Of late-day study hall, keeping peace
Among one hundred and twenty students.

That doctor, the caption says, stared at the skulls
Of strangers, followed men to their homes,
And wrote down addresses as if they were
Inside information for wagers.
And me? One night I followed that teacher
To his house for drinks in his living room
Where the furniture matched in muted plaid,
The drapes a green so dark I believed them black
Until his wife explained how their color myrtle
Set off the chairs and couch. Before I left,
He replaced my bottles in a slotted case

Because he only bought returnables,
The thick brown glass shielding the beer from light.
And then his wife, with a voice that rustled,
Said "See you later" as if the words
Shuffled pages in a magazine,
Following me outside, her breath white
In the late September night, hugging herself
In the cold as if she lived alone,
Less than a month until he beat her to death
In that immaculate house I passed
Each morning and afternoon, pulling,
At last, into the driveway of crushed stones,
Hearing six cars go by behind me
While I watched as if I expected movement,
The drapes pulled shut, the windows darkened
Like a closed display, my hands, despite myself,
Lifting to my face, reading like the blind
Before I looked into the mirror where
My single set of tracks retreated
To the highway through week-old snow.

The Shelter Revival

After decades of disrepair,
All but the crazy deserting
Their underground rooms, bomb shelters
Are back, anxiety salesmen
Pitching luxurious bunkers,
Communities for the cautious
Who can afford survival, sites
In several states and growing.
They're versatile now, more to fear
Than a massive nuclear launch.
They're built to endure comet strike,
Supervolcano, solar flare,
And the infinitesimal
Risk of brown dwarf star intrusion.
Tsunami pods, tornado-proof
Pyramids, old missile silos
Refurbished by squatters who share
The language of weather and time
And probability rote-learned
The way we studied every subject
When those silos were constructed—
State capitals, the times tables,
Presidents and Pennsylvania
Counties beginning with Adams
And Allegheny, where we lived
Less than a mile from where the world
Would begin to end, the missiles
Ascending and vanishing while
Sirens spoke our earliest words
To drive us to prayer, the cover
Of basements, or the privacy
Of secret shelters where neighbors

Would be huddled like the eyeless,
Outliving us by captive weeks,
My father insisting we were
Lucky to live close to defense,
Those silos hidden like ancient
Mine shafts, missiles reliable
As crocuses, their purple surprise
Surfacing so early in March
We were always astonished, snow
Still staggering in thin flurries
Like residue of aftermath,
Our shoes churning old mulch into
The dark smear of apocalypse.

The Infinity Room

Last month, after weeks of delays and a background check
and the five-hour coach flight to Las Vegas, I boarded
a tourist bus and rode sixty-five miles to the stop,
halfway to an A-bomb test site, for a security search,
cell phones and cameras as taboo as guns.
Another hour and we were beside the scar of Shot Sedan,
its crater a quarter-mile wide, a hundred yards deep,
the bomb, one morning, exploded just beneath the earth
because someone proposed it an efficient way to excavate.
Everybody's questions were childlike. A woman leaned
close to tell me she had never felt so unimportant.
We drank water from plastic bottles, no one bareheaded.
When one man shielded his eyes, the guide said, "Dark glasses,"
as if they were on sale nearby or likely to be found,
a pair left behind or intact for over half a century.

In Harrisburg, yesterday, a college friend said, *vitrification*
like a password or clue, the two of us standing across
the Susquehanna from Three Mile Island, and yet
I answered, "What?" as if touring a test site had
taught me nothing. The worst nuclear waste, he said,
is melted with glass beads in furnaces and poured into
steel boxes to become blocks of radioactive glass.
A plane approaching the nearby airport seemed to be
sightseeing the two quiet towers. With proper care,
he went on, those bricks will outlast the sun, nodding
across the river, nothing in his gesture suggesting debate.

Retired, he has moved to South Carolina, where
reprocessing canyons have been built to house
those furnaces, where radioactive remains, in bulk,
have been shipped for burial. Early that morning

he had attended church in my Pennsylvania town,
keeping the faith despite his doctorate in physics.
In the newspaper was a history of Silly Putty as sidebar
to an article on the government's search for landfills,
the full-time job of deciding what's under our feet.
My friend noticed that my county's map was shaded
with live sites. "It's indestructible," the paper's expert
proclaimed, ten million pounds of that gunk in landfills, lakes
and the basements of abandoned houses, saying how,
because the putty mimics the specific gravity of our flesh,
we empathize with the probable permanence of toys.

Outside, my German shepherd dug near the forsythia border,
attacking a spot where something delicious must hide.

"Forever and ever, world without end, amen," I said,
and though my friend didn't argue, he told me that once,
at Rocky Flats, where plutonium detonators were made,
one chamber became so contaminated it was called
the Infinity Room for how long it would be poisonous.
Needing a story of my own, I said I'd lived, once,
across the street from a veteran who'd marched,
under orders the following day, to Sedan's ground zero.
"My sixteenth birthday!" I'd exclaimed like a fool,
and whether polite or not hearing me, that soldier said,
"That goddamned fucking bomb took years to kill me," so thin
by then he looked devoured when he walked his small dog
just after dawn to our cul-de-sac's grass island.
Always, before he returned, his wife opened their drapes,
spreading them with her hands instead of pulling the cord.
As if she were impatient for welcoming the light
that I imagined could cast his narrow shadow upon her.

Until it's buried, everything tells us we're important.
I cranked up the window to shout, "Find something!"
but that dog was intent on exposing the planet,
the hole in the lawn staying empty so long I thought
it would widen until my house tumbled to fill it.
Both of us watched the dog while my friend recounted how,
in medieval medical histories, there are illustrations of doctors'
birdlike masks with red glass eyewear to ward off evil,
the beaks full of herbs and spices to combat the foul air
that carried death. Surely, he said, that sweetness did
not purge the plague, but those patients, their boils
swelling, must have regretted their own bare faces.
Outside, the wind rose enough to make me check the sky
for approaching clouds. Look, he went on, somebody's job is
to create warning signs that will still make sense to people
in South Carolina twenty thousand years from now.
Think of not understanding those symbols and seeing
the doctors in hazmat suits, noting how carefully each one
carries himself and his calibrated machinery, the air
so clear you are astonished, even as their hidden eyes
confirm that safety has fled like prudent neighbors.

The Startling Language of Shriveling Leaves

This week, three socks slip into unpaired comas,
Sleep with the clean and useless in drawers
While the cryonicists have flown in like angels.

We sat rapt through their singing, the cantatas
Of our chilled cells repaired, one by one,
Mutinied to health and youth by computer.

Our old photographs are bleeding like icons.
They are listening while we compare
The ransom demands of resurrections.

Look here, I murmur this morning, pulling off
The just-widened highway. A white sock,
A brown, a blue—they are enough to stir us

To trust walk, no other laundry for miles,
As if someone has seeded the shoulder
To set us to searching like test mice.

We watch boredom's scenery—cinders, tar,
Roadside weeds indecipherable as deeds—
And wish for small skeletons, ruptured bodies,

And flattened fur. You declare nothing should be
So laundered, not even the highway
Upon which only official tires have spun.

An arm's-length swath of green-going-brown follows
The guardrail where the county has sprayed.
Sumac collapses. The poison ivy burns.

Together we listen until we hear
The startling language of shriveling leaves
And the careful chorus of our clothing.

Preserving Cursive

This late afternoon I am one of three
Supporting the teacher who's advertised
An action group for preserving cursive.
In an adjoining room, a support group
For the parents of daughters with eating
Disorders, those who, hour by hour,
Inspect the penmanship of their bodies
As if they are graded according to
The Peterson method for perfect script.

Because we are harmless, the teacher turns
Her back to write beautifully upon
The blackboard. Your handwriting reveals you
To the world, she says, and though I believe
What reveals is the exact arrangement
Of the words I choose, I am astonished
By the symmetry of her sample lines.

My grandmother, for years, told me how,
If we concentrated, we would receive
Correspondence from heaven, that the saved
Could be prompted by prayer to send letters
In handwriting we could identify.
My mother, the secretary, could write
Perfectly in longhand and shorthand, loops
And slants exactly the same from message
To message. For decades, she kept the books
For my father's bakery, entering
Purchases in cursive so clear I could,
Ten years after her death, identify
Every product like an auditor.

There is a moment, driving home in rain,
When I wish for the commitment to be
Missionary for anything, even
The antiquated notion of cursive
Or the way the King James Bible sounded
So much like the voice of God because of
The anachronistic and obsolete.

My mother, just hours before her death,
Wrote me a letter running three pages
Before she admitted she'd never felt
So nauseous, acknowledging kidney
Failure in perfect cursive, that letter
Arriving the day after burial
As if it were postmarked from paradise.

For twenty-six years, in calligraphy,
My poem about her death hung framed and
Under glass in my father's living room.
Each time I visited, before he closed
His eyes and faced away, he asked me to
Proofread while he recited thirty-one
Soft lines, confirming one small perfection.

The Lost Continents

Except for the last owners who stall the arrival
        of eminent domain,
Everyone has died or forgotten about this avenue
        of porches and chairs
Not packed, not all of them, by the old women who sit
        to shame the bulldozers.
And what can I say, accidental visitor, to three
        of them settled in front
Of sooty windows where a future of double lanes
        will please commuters?
That *ruin* is a prelude for developers, *forgetting*
        the great synonym
For improvement? In the wrecker's nearest empty lot
        I scrape my shoes
And say nothing about the nostalgia of men who search
        for countries sunk miles
Beneath the oceans, not settling for Atlantis,
        so serious about
Our storybook origins, someone, not far from this street,
        finances a search
For Lemuria, the lost continent of the Indian Ocean.
        I say nothing
About the men who want to set the winch of wishful thinking
        to the weight of Mu,
Raise that shipwrecked world from deep in the Pacific
        for possible treasure.
Rocking in their wicker chairs, Mrs. Bondula and her sister
        might listen to me,
The aging neighborhood boy, say those are two more sites
        for the Garden of Eden
And fossils fortunate to belief. That while they dry, while
        those new continents

Open to the migration of seeds and birds, our children
        are driving over
A thousand sites of lost things to arrive at the rented rooms
        of personal history,
Their children, in turn, repeating "What?" as they marvel
        and brush themselves
Like the lucky at crash sites, listening to the old tales
        of emigration when
The oceans, accordingly, rose, when the displaced seas
        sloshed up the coasts
With the perpetual dreams of bonding that suggest
        someone will surely
Translate a prophecy scrawled in the waterproof words
        of a mother tongue,
Someone verifying its age to refute the skeptics,
        someone funding
Search after search for a swath of definitive relics while
        the world moves inland
To begin the long wait for the resurrected landscape.
        Just now, these widows
Named Florence and Pearl and Heloise are singing
        the ancient round
Of *What's Happened*? So let me listen to them saying,
        "You'll see someday,"
In the terse tongue of the experienced. Let me enter
        the shops posted
Everything Must Go to buy one of everything
        in a gesture
Of tiny, fruitless charity. Let me carry away
        a miscellany
Of hand-painted animals, a dozen antique beer cans
        for a basement shelf.

Let me sit for shoe repair, stumble on the sudden lift
        of unworn heels
Before my hair is trimmed and oiled by the barber
        who's been doing
Crossword puzzles all day. Let me climb the steep street
        to the overlook
Soon to be blasted. Let me balance on the guardrail
        that has borne my name
And the names of a thousand children who signed
        the low, public wall
Of romanticism. Let me step up to teeter over
        everything about
To be buried. And let me challenge my balance
        while I memorize

The landfill where our descendants will test that mud
        of possible heaven,
And, whether settled or not, excavate its shale for the bones
        of paradise,
Traveling, if they discover nothing, to the next
        long-buried town,
Carrying the cumulative fear of faith to dive for
        the lost world not yet named.

The Secret City

Ed Westcott was the twenty-ninth employee hired for the Manhattan Project in Oak Ridge. He was the official government photographer there from 1942 to 1966.

PHOTO #1: THE PERENNIALS OF OAK RIDGE

The trellises are handmade, vines
And branches trained upward, beauty
And comfort compatible, though
Temporary and brief like each

Sad emphasis on hope no one
Speaks of until privacy returns.
Inside laboratories, riddles
Whispered, answers unsolvable

As the equation for heaven.
The stems climb their small increments
Of reassurance, leaves opening
To drink up the light like addicts.

Annuals have been abandoned
Like promises of surrender.
In this second summer, fast-climbing
Perennials. Possible, now, to

Believe in the sensuality
Of shadows cast by the rise of roses,
The ascension of morning glories,
Or, at least, the small contentment

Of latticework that amplifies

The spell of early evening before
Descending light diffuses into
The indifferent drift to darkness.

Always, throughout the war, the flawless guards
demand photo IDs, no exceptions.

PHOTO #2: SANTA CLAUS ARRIVES AT OAK RIDGE
Santa's made the trip by automobile.
He's working day shift, the reindeer pastured,
But his Chevrolet is stopped like a spy's.
Although Santa ho-hos, the guards remain
In character, serious as war while
They rummage through two sacks, reminding him
The red flag of his baggy suit requires
A pat-down, including his shiny boots.

He's scuffling now, stumbling like a hobo,
That sack unwieldy with stocking stuffers,
Footing uncertain on the unpaved street
As irregular as pieces of coal
Meant to terrify the worst brat polite.
By the time he's surrounded by children,
He's a mess of mud splatter, gasping brief
White clouds like the ones the reindeer pant when
The sleigh is miraculously loaded.

Housewives on Saturdays, the mothers have
Made an hour among their chores. They've dressed
For Santa Claus, the secret work of war
Set aside like a long novel, the place

Bookmarked by a small child's crayoned drawing—
The stick figures of family and pets,
An oval sun whose beams strafe house and yard.

Near Santa's hardback throne, consequence lifts
Like tentative fog; the children form lines
From the left and right, loud but orderly.
The mothers retreat. Cameras taboo,
They memorize the scene like poetry:
The bright marathon of wishful thinking,
Footballs and bicycles, dolls and board games,
Roller skates and air rifles and all those
Perfectly detailed model Air Force planes.

> *Six beauty shops, two bakeries. Never*
> *counted, tens of thousands of ashtrays.*

PHOTO #3: THE MIDTOWN FIRES, 1944
During the invasion
Of January, the year begins

With the flickering firefights
Of uncertain outcome.

Trailer flames, hutment blazes—
Every neighborhood in Oak Ridge

Lights up the epidemic year,
Nearly a thousand alarms

Despite the trained caution

Of every resident.

An hour or more, each night,
Some lie awake like watchmen

For the burglary of fire.
Children are slapped, sometimes,

For carelessness. Out of love.
Out of inevitability.

Someone's hands always shake
Over kerosene, the fuel so

Necessary, the inexperienced
Are forced to defuse.

As if daily sacrifice was required
By the American version of God.

As if the trailers were set
On altars fashioned by faith,

The temporary triumph of flame
Across a street or distant

As an accidental Passover,
The fortunate rising

To reignite before walking
To incomprehensible work

With discipline, resignation,
And yes, with joy.

> *Without preference, the chapel serves all*
> *the Protestant sects, Catholics, and Jews.*

PHOTO #4: SQUARE THROUGH IN OAK RIDGE
Each Saturday night, in Oak Ridge, Bill Pierce
Calls squares for workers out for a good time
At the Midtown Rec Hall. Comfortable
Or clumsy, the couples keep following
His lead. How quickly the city women
Have learned from rural friends, but their men are
As reluctant as boys at a school dance.
Do-si-do, Bill calls, now four ladies chain.
Behind him the fiddler has time to slip
In a pinch of chew tobacco. Later,
He has a sad solo when the dance turns
Slow and private, but now it's the simple
Refrains, the sound of shuffling and laughter
As Pierce works old-timey into his calls:
Hey, all join hands and circle to the south,
And get a little moonshine in your mouth.

This night, Pierce switches to wartime patter:
Now allemande left with a soldier's wife.
If we finish our work, we'll save his life.
The fiddler tells Pierce he misread a gauge
Into red. Thankfully, correctible,
The danger brief and only to himself.
Luck is singing with a fiddle and bow.

All move together now, and do-si-do.
Right now there's time enough to celebrate
The unraveling of whatever's feared,
A near-rhyme for urgency's solitaire
With a single, mysterious lab task.
Pierce calls three familiar couplets to close,
And the fiddler holds the last note, then bows,
The necessity of the smallest share;
Any larger, impossible to bear.

> *In all of the dorms of the Secret City,*
> *the ironing rooms were for women only.*

PHOTO #5: HUTMENTS COME TO OAK RIDGE
In Oak Ridge, races are separated
At the gate by the planned simplicity
Of expectations, the Negroes packed off
To hutments in Gamble Valley, their jobs
Requiring nothing more than dirty hands,
Heavy lifting, and huge humility.
Hutments, they learn, are sixteen by sixteen
Packing boxes, in each wall, one window
Without glass or screens, boards available
To shut out flies, mosquitoes, rain, and light.
What's more, Negro husbands are not allowed
To live with wives, and though they visit each
Other like prisoners, in the evenings
The wives are widows, the nights as formless
As Genesis. So it's no surprise that
More than half the Negroes refuse those cells,
Choose to commute daily from Knoxville, but

Always, like migrants, driven in by bus,
Rebroken like badly set, fractured bones,
Searched each morning for weapons, contraband,
The remnants of reasons not to obey.
Always, through the translucent, stained windows,
They watch the guards gather as if woken
By alarms set so low in frequency,
They seem to insist from within like pulse.

Gaseous diffusion plant κ25 was, during the war,
the world's largest building under one roof.

PHOTO #6: THE TRAVELING LIBRARY IN OAK RIDGE, 1946
The children are eager for more pictures.
They scramble for warriors and princesses
Who will sometimes meet and love each other
Before or during or after battles.

Illustrated or not, none of the books
Mentions Oak Ridge, where those children's parents
Have begun to learn how they ended war
With obedience, discipline, and care.

Because science is a workday subject,
Because research never ends, these children
Will remain three years yet before the gates
Will open, all of them with time to learn

The new definition of infinite.
One of the boys is returning a book
Of horses, its gold-bordered cover torn

Through two pintos whose faces his mother

Has taped while he sobbed out apology.
Now, before the librarian reshelves
Those horses into circulation, she
Inspects for the interior damage

Of marginal notes, things scribbled as code.
Satisfied, she runs her finger along
The tape before pressing it to the boy's
Damp forehead as if she were knighting him.

> *Cattle exposed to fallout from the A-bomb test*
> *in Socorro were shipped to Oak Ridge for study.*

PHOTO #7: THE NEW MEXICO CATTLE, 1946

What's striking, at first, is that every cow
Inside this rough-hewn corral is facing
The camera, curious as just-found
Political prisoners. Slatted fencing
Reveals an open landscape unlike where
Those cattle absorbed the consequences
Of the first atomic bomb. Scientists
Are listening to *Inevitable's*
Preliminary report. Everything
They observe and record is essential,
Vital work, heavy with imperatives.
Not one of them has ever touched a cow,
But now they will keep them, especially
The yearling in the foreground who confirms

There is no limit to our emptiness.

After the war. Oak Ridge watched its story
At the Grove—"The Beginning or the End?"

PHOTO #8: THE GIRL SCOUTS VISIT OAK RIDGE, 1951
In full uniform, neckerchiefs and hats,
The Girl Scouts enter what's billed as sacred,
But the roads are unpaved, and though it's June,
They're muddy from recent rain, the ruts filled
With standing water, the ridges gooey.

The story ends, they all know, the summer
Before they started school, the final year
August didn't swirl toward apprehension.
Their leader, this morning, has related
How, during her junior year, the high school
Closed over Christmas vacation, saying,
"Just like that. No warning. Disappeared. Gone."

Look, right now they are afraid for their shoes,
Or worse, the misery of sudden slip.
The tour is just beginning, and Miss Spatz
Would never excuse anyone, not when
They have traveled thirteen miles, not after
The careful arrangements for permission
To examine, firsthand, where the world changed.

Half of the girls love Frank Sinatra; half
Have been raised on Hank Williams. Four of them
Have televisions with snow-plagued channels

In their houses, and one has a father
Who tracks the frequency of A-bomb tests
In Nevada, the site remote as Mars.

Russians, he's said, know the end-time secrets.
For Christmas, her mother gave her dancing
Lessons; for her birthday, she renewed them
Like a subscription. When water covers
Her ankle, she leaps and squeals like science.

ii.

The Absolute

To have a tour guide is an absolute
No one disbelieves. Everybody stays
On the sidewalks. As if the Earth were flat,
The abyss swarming with microseiverts.
For years now, Chernobyl has residents
Who have returned to acceptable risk,
The infamous reactor miles away,
The pair of unfinished ones paused beside
Cranes poisoned for a hundred centuries.

It's Pripyat where nobody chances
A souvenir, where an amusement park,
Nine days from opening, is forever
Poised to start Ferris wheel and bumper cars.

None of its 50,000 can come back,
Except, in April, for one day per year,
Something like a reunion, permitted
To visit the deserted to see that
A version of everything that they were
Continues without them. The young, we're told,
Re-enter with their parents, use that day
To drink in the ruins, to break what's left.

After the Bomb Drill, Miss Hartung Teaches Weather

You think weather is unremarkable?
All this year where the worst is minus ten
And tornadoes are news from Ohio?
We've had school every day, not one delay,
But don't be fooled. Sit up now, and listen.
In less than a day, sixty-eight inches of rain
Have fallen, and the fastest foot of rain,
Forty-two minutes, was in Missouri,
Not far. In July, a blizzard has swept
The Plains; for Christmas Eve, in Montana,
A drop of eighty-four degrees, and you
In your flimsy jackets, thinking winter
Takes a holiday like this little school.

The weather forecast is for clouds. Don't interrupt.
There's no telling what else might be coming.
Be prepared. Those Boy Scouts don't know the half
Of it. Sit around until the night sky
Goes noon-bright. Trust me, your fathers will hide
Inside their closets like house-fire children.
In the worst of weather, you're on your own.
You know what I'm talking about, don't you?
Next time be quiet; next time, most of all,
Keep your eyes shut until I say *open*.

The Nuclear Age

1

At Stonehenge, the Head Groundsman trims
The lawn with a push mower like the one
My father says is mine, at twelve, to use
When needed, on our patch of grass.

Across the street, in June, a man
Who lived by himself had died. My father,
In July, ordered me to mow the lawn
Of the dead that, all along, had harbored
Thistle, goldenrod, and milkweed.

2

At Stonehenge, the Head Groundsman rolls
Up the sleeves of his white oxford, a shirt
Like the one I wear only on Sundays,
Freshly washed, starched and ironed.

That summer the Bible became a book
Of stories. Church was a chore poorly done.
Everything will outlive me, I wrote
In the journal of my body. On each page,
Alone, I undressed and imagined joy.

3

At Stonehenge, the Head Groundsman loves
His ancient church. He trims the base
Of the miraculous construction,
Meticulous in each shadow.

Late October, when I walked the mower
Into the garage, my father explained

Exactly where to store it for winter,
And for the first time, I felt the sadness
Earned from the privacy of work.

4

At Stonehenge, the Head Groundsman fluffs
His thinning hair. His work, my father says,
Is like ours, his future the constant care
For the solitary maintenance of faith.

One Sunday I read about the villages
Abandoned in the Soviet Union,
The ones whose names had been erased from maps.
Even then, I knew the villagers were dead
Or dying in places inexplicable

As radiation or relics visited
By tourists who listen for the ghosts
Of significance that must surround them
In a clean, well-tended cathedral.

Upon the Tongue

This morning, two weeks into
A regimen of painkillers
And antibiotics, I'm thinking
Of Luisa Piccarreta, who ate
Only communion wafers,
Feeding on medicinal doses
To fight the sicknesses of sin.

I'm remembering the way
I was instructed to accept
Those wafers upon my tongue—
Hold them, don't chew—until
They softened sufficiently
To easily swallow
That brief diet of remorse.

And I'm wondering, right now,
How she felt between meals
When hunger made her sick
Of promises, because yesterday,
Driving between exits spaced
More than forty miles apart
On a limited access highway,
Pain forced me to dry-mouth
An emergency dose, and I gagged
On relief so urgent I bit
That pill and chewed, swallowing
The tiny paste of prayer,
Preparing to admit nothing
About necessity, whatever
Else was gathering to flourish.

While I Am Standing

Off Houston, down Bowery, at Second,
Where men arrange a hundred metal carts
For the hot dog and pretzel vendors
Of New York, a man believes he will draw
His savings from my daughter's window
If a teller would raise her iron bars.
Three hundred dollars, he wants. Not much,
But Christ, he shouts, this bank is refusing
Him the price of a transplanted heart.
He checks his ring of keys, poking them,
One by one, at my daughter's outside door.
Seventeen, he tries, counting, but when
My daughter opens that door, he backs off
From her white shepherd and shoves a key
Into my van's locked door. "I've killed a man,"
He says. "I'll have a heart attack by noon."
Some place inside of something is where
His money is, but half a block from us
Two girls cross the street, and a woman lifts
Her baby from a stroller as if she
Has chosen this moment for the rapture
Of touching. He pulls that key and pivots
Into the weed-filled, overgrown lot next door.
He says, "Another step, sister, and I'm
Gonna kill that dog," and I can't tell
If he means to use hands or house keys.
My daughter's white shepherd strains its chain.
A torn poster flaps against its feet,
A jazz benefit, the sad faces
Of orphaned children wrapping around
Its right front paw. "Gonna kill it, sweetheart.
Send it straight up to our righteous God,"

He says, holding those keys as if they could
Open a throat. Across from him a truck
Double parks the striped delivery zone
For pushcarts. The driver opens his door,
And I imagine that whatever will
Stop this man's faulty heart has started, all
Of us walking the tiny wilderness
Of inevitable horror, thick grass
Bent and stirred, then suddenly standing still.

The Light

How often is the light erased?

The waiting room is half full
of eyes damaged to specialized care,
those paired for post-visit rides,
marriages made by need,
whether shadows, sparkles, haze,
or the closing panels of darkness.

Can you name the ways?

From diabetes, Robert Godfrey,
whose glasses were as dark
as each pair I wished for
in my daily dream of cool.
By macular degeneration
in the eyes of Emma Hemmerline,
who was always seated early,
last pew by the window that featured
Christ surrounded by a flock of doves.

Did you count ignorance and indifference?

Yes, my ineptitude with tools,
the refrain of no, not that way, no.
The eyes of three women, then
another, said absence, their voices
carrying like a stage whisper.

What about betrayal?

When failed promises align

like a full solar eclipse,
they can be examined, but
they will extinguish the light.

Are there more? Have you seen them?

Glaucoma was Major Hartman, who dressed
in uniform each Sunday, never
using a white cane. Who took a stance
near the curb, looking at the vocal
while I waited for my father, who
found me so late, some days, the sidewalk
was free of men in white shirts and ties,
leaving Major Hartman to pivot
before trailing the staccato line
of his sister's reliable heels.

What about the sighted?

Fourteen years ago, my neighbor
kept me awake for what he said
was rare and incredible.
At last, an hour past midnight,
Jupiter disappeared behind the moon.
Not again, he said, until 2026.
Not again, I said, in our lifetime.

What about the unseen?

From tumors.
From meningitis.
From birth defects.

From chemical burns.
From secrets well kept.

What about sixty-five years of the commonplace?

My father said glasses would disqualify me
from manhood, and yes, I nodded like a servant.

My father, proud of his eyesight, named birds only
at distances far enough to require my faith.

Oriole, he said, cardinal, goldfinch, speaking
as if he were the census taker for heaven.

And when I cried "sick," excusing myself from church,
he cited Saul transformed on the Damascus road,

as if my plummeting eyesight came precisely
from a God who might pick me for a change of name.

What about now?

The ophthalmologist, this morning,
confirms cataracts like appointments.
Immature, he says, let them ripen,
what you have here so ordinary,
everyone who lives long enough
will have them. My wife, driving home,
says, "The best you could hope for,"
meaning it's like remission,
daylight flooding my treated eyes.

What about then?

The storm of retreating light.
The body a burden.
My father's interrogation by silence,
His assumptions by grimace.
A year's work was brooding
and the determination to sleep.

What about now?

The world is a face of mouths.

Is this inexhaustible?

At eighty, my father,
refusing glasses, turned
into a curb, bending
an axle. At eighty-one,
he drove over a rock
that gashed his gas tank,
a trail following two miles
to his driveway. "Look,"
a neighbor said. "See?"
and walked my father
down the street, speaking
in his kindest voice.
Without repair, the car was
towed and sold. For nine years,
the driveway sat clear,
the garage abandoned
to the discarded.

The Rain after Sunrise

The falling-away, grandmother says, can
Be cured by rain, as long as the shower
Is caught before sunrise. In that water,
She says, boil an egg. Through its shell, bore
Three holes, then set it upon an anthill
And wait for the hunger of ants to end
Weakness, weight loss, or persistent decline.

Like all of the dead, she repeats herself,
Sometimes shaking me awake in the dark
To say it's raining, to suggest an egg.
Pay attention, she says, there are hundreds
Of versions of falling-away, the skin
And bones, the heart's flicker, the mute surprise
At the cloudless noon of embolism.

And lately, there are evenings of weakness,
A daily log of general decline.
A vague pressure turns to pain and swelling.
In the kitchen, the bleak jingle of knives.
Upstairs, my daughter showers for so long
I worry that she's fainted. One son flicks
Through ninety channels. My wife is speaking

To twenty-four children who have inhaled
Household products to alter an hour.
Outside, the late morning rain compresses
The anthill near the crown vetch to the cyst
Of a child's castle swirled sodden by tide,
Bubbles forming in the sand's needled holes
To show something alive lies beneath them.

The Secret Voice

While sleeping in the room
Given to me, for three months
By a friend, I startled up
From nightmare, crying aloud.
A half hour, it took, to settle
And trust the reality
Of those walls. In the morning,
With coffee, my friend watched news
While I ate cereal that soaked
In borrowed milk. He didn't ask
About my work, my family,
Or the cry he'd likely heard.
His wife gave me clipped coupons,
Discounts on fast food I ate
For lunch and dinner because
I wouldn't take charity
For more than a room and milk.
That nightmare showed the nearby
River about to swallow me,
My car airborne and plunging
Until I screamed the secret voice
That was mine for when I needed
To be saved, lying in the dark,
The drapes as tightly closed
As a foregone conclusion
Followed by footsteps that could have
Been my friend, his wife, or either
Of his two daughters pausing
Like held breath in the hallway,
Choosing between terror and desire.

Stunned

Sometimes, I've learned, the eyes of birds
Weigh more than their brains. Sometimes
Their bones weigh less than their feathers.

Sometimes, while touching her face,
I became a boy who believed
Her eyes exclaimed, "Yes, go on,"

Because, undressed, she felt so light
Her luminous body lifted
Toward me, extraordinary

As the moment she became
An etched inscription on a plaque—
She was, she loved, she would have—

An odd conjugation of loss,
A wound in the air placed within
The private museum of the past

Just beyond the corridor
For longing where light is absorbed,
Where flight is interrupted

By the undeniable
Levitation of accident.

A Blanket Was over Her Body

Say your teacher has beaten his wife to death.
Say both of them were elderly, long retired.
That three weeks before, he had suffered a stroke,
Depending upon her until he hated
Each moment of concern in her hospice voice,
Becoming a person of interest, not
A convalescing invalid, not helpless.
Say the police, during their press conference,
Repeat how frail the teacher is, recall
How, decades ago, he taught them to drive,
Reminding them, always, to use turn signals,
Not as courtesy, but to follow the law.

Know he's not the teacher who took your daughter
To breakfast, then asked her again before she
Told you. Not the teacher who raped your daughter's
Babysitter, saying her breasts were "perfect."
Know the house is two blocks from where your children
Were small, a Halloween stop the years of ghosts,
Ninja Turtles, and the small two-headed girl
Knocking where the crabapple border blossoms
This week, fat rows of pink shading daffodils
You admire—*Landscape with Killer's House*—weapon
Not yet assigned a name for what yields blunt force
Trauma to chest and shoulders, the neck and head.

Remember the way the previous owners
Of your first house had repaired three bullet holes,
The wife willing to bargain when you loitered
In her kitchen, her husband become photos
In her bedroom, displayed at the scene like clues.
Remember there were years of your dimpled wall

59

Matching the butt end of your cue stick; the years
Of a dog skittering and silent, that house,
After its third year of damage, sold "as is."
Remember, now, to be thankful for your house
Of flawless walls, the cue sticks arranged by length
And weight, table brushed and covered like the past.

Say there are evenings when you are so ugly
With motive and memory that you become
Afraid to speak, shy with fear of confessing
The thousand phrases for anger, for brutal,
Each morning a small pledge taken with water.
Know the dead's been carried from the teacher's house,
Not yours, where never hasn't arrived, not yet,
Exhausted, maybe, by long foreshadowing:
Cue stick and handgun, the unidentified.
Remember there's no difference between silence
And speech, that community, for order, forms
The ephemeral church of understanding.

Merging, Slowing, the Second Sun

> *Plants may be black on planets with more than one sun.*
>
> —Harper's

In 1953,
to test the effects of fallout,
the army sprayed toxic chemicals
from the back of a truck driven
past a Minneapolis grade school.
That year, my friends and I, near
Pittsburgh, walked to second grade
inside a coal-smoke cloud, passing
the blocks-long Spang-Chalfant mill
where the light and heat of molten steel
poured over us like the weather
in one comic book we'd shared,
a second sun drifting toward Earth
as panels filled with sweating people
and children crying for water.

In the end cactus ruled, scorpions
scuttling on a planet of sand,
but none of us, for decades, learned
about the army's experiment,
the reason I'm thinking hard
about the early reunions
of that Minneapolis school,
the women talking miscarriage
and stillbirth, the men concealing
unlikely cancers, everybody
young in their misery while,
over drinks, my friends and I

compared photos of our children,
outlasting the darkened mills.

Now, more than sixty years elapsed,
everyone from either school
can see seventy approaching
like an improbable sun,
all of us remembering when
we believed every teacher
to be a minister or priest
until we learned to be serious
about news particular to ourselves.
For instance, this morning's lead story
about the suspect landfill beneath
our playground, its poisons edited
from government reports ten years
and counting, leaving us with worry.

Or this car radio bulletin
about a woman found, piece by piece,
in eight twist-and-tied black bags strewn
beside this state-run thruway as if
sprouted toward an unnatural sky
from a forgotten garden.
Meaning, as I drive three women
who trust me, we merge to one lane,
slowing, and creep past six policemen
with leashed dogs. Meaning, all of us
stare while I try not to imagine
each one-eighth of their bodies
and what, in Pennsylvania, might
be tested to save them from such crime.

Worship

After a student's accidental death,
Her teacher, by hand, copies her poem
About the possibilities of love,
Reforming the imagery for desire
With intricate loops and decisive lines.

    In Covington, Kentucky, on the grounds
    Of a Benedictine monastery,
    The monks built Monte Casino, forming,
    From limestone, the world's tiniest chapel.

Her setting is the garden of St. Paul
Tended by two ancient nuns who, each day,
Inspect the light altered by arrangements
Of decorative trees, who prune, monthly,
The rose bushes to allow kneeling for
The raised right hand of a smiling Mary.

    Six feet by nine, cell-sized, our group is told.
    Maximum occupancy three, a pew
    For each of us as if the secret phrase
    Is "save yourself," mote-swirled haze seeping through.

Her lines are a gospel of surfaces,
Touch by touch where nerves nearly breach the skin.
They detail the sacrificial blossoms,
The needy topiary that shadows
The deep erosions from September's storms.

    The single leaded window, the belfry
    Above too small for bells, and though we know

A smaller church has recently been built
On a deck in the center of a pond,

And then, at last, shifting to a statue
Of the garden saint, his blessed hand smooth
From centuries of kisses, her poem
Ending in an astonishment of prayer.

We study the history of this church,
The monks moving on, replaced by vandals,
And yet salvaged, brought here and restored, now
Lovingly tended for our tiny joy.

The Sum Total

Beware the sum total, a thing that bites,
Miss Sussex said, sounding like a pastor.
Children, we all are numbers, just listen,
Reading us Bible words, speaking for God.

The sum total growled, teeth bared, when columns
Of figures covered the church's blackboard,
And Miss Sussex called us up and offered
Thirty seconds to work out an answer

Like one thousand, two hundred eighty-four,
The sum total of eight numbers, then nine,
Then ten, carrying ones and twos and threes
While everybody waited for a turn,

From Ronald Ambrose to Anthony Zeck,
Who clutched the white chalk and panicked, scribbling
A guess so terrible Miss Sussex pressed
A finger to her lips to warn us mute.

Children, Miss Sussex said, yes, all of you,
Don't kid yourselves, the sum total can be
Zero, or worse yet, somewhere far below
Where the ordinary can be counted,

The negatives I said nothing about,
The private additions of greed and lies,
Jealousy, laziness, and lack of faith.
So far below zero, so self-absorbed,

I thought my secrecy was singular,
Saying my sums without moving my lips

Like Frank Wertz, who whispered the numbers one
Through six before he opened his Bible;

The sum total twenty-one to finish
One tiny routine while I imagined
The sum total of eternity that
Pounces at the sudden end of numbers.

The Lengthening Radius for Hate: A Sequence

KENT, OHIO

I sat, one morning, on the grass
Where years before I'd survived
The guardsmen's volley. I sprawled
Beside a parking lot so long
I wondered why nobody
Questioned me. I could see the small,
Stone memorial to four dead
Students, the pagoda unchanged
On the hill's horizon. What was
I expecting while I became
My grandfather walking the mile
Of his lost mill where strikebreakers
Succeeded once, then failed? Became
My father crossing the landfilled
Lot of his long-closed bakery
And recalling the gunman who thought
Robbing him would change his life.
Something stood here and then was gone—
Furnaces, ovens, armed men in gas masks,
The work we did from steel to bread
To books. I told myself I'd sit
Until somebody asked me why,
And morning slid past noon, women
And men moving to cars, pulling
Away, unwilling to answer.

THE FIRE LANDSCAPE

Across the street, across the tracks and creek.
Across the cindered lot to where slag piles
Rose higher than the three second-floor rooms
We rented, Spang-Chalfant dumped heaps of flame.

From our unheated attic, my mother
Holding her breath and me, I leaned, some nights,
Through the small window's stick-propped space to see.
Downstairs, space heaters glowed the red patterns
Of fire waffles. Two radiators hissed
And drooled and waited for the touch that made
Me suck away the sudden pain of sin.
In the cellar was a coal-fired furnace.
Below it was the open hearth of hell.

Tonight, it's the flammable that matters,
This myth of myself that tests the closed door
For a secret blaze, sniffs like a dog dazed
By strangers. The house expands before sleep;
Room after room is careless with clutter.
Nothing is trustworthy. The radio
Hides embers; the night light is open flame.
I've listened to the saints of nails and glass,
The saints of bitterness, the saints of blood.
I've become the saint of appliances,
Dreaming about twisted cords, waking to
The imminent squeal of smoke alarms from
Short circuits, from insulation gone wrong,
From overheating, exhausts clogged by lint.

So many plugs to pull, switches to check,
The shift, by inches, of things from sources
Of heat, all this penance for mistrusting
Others in the common complaint of doubt.
My mother searched each room before leaving.
Never once, she said, had she forgotten,
Not even a low-watt bathroom light bulb.

Some nights my father would drive us north where
Farms were turning into streets of houses,
Each lot a chance I'd live among children
Who thought steel was dug from the ground like coal.
When we moved, my room was so black I dreamed
Myself dead, woke and went to my window
Where the darkness convinced me I was right,
And I stopped breathing, waiting to see where
I was traveling, toward which kind of light.

WOOM! BALL

We circled at 3 a.m., just before the two-mile run, fifteen pledges who
slammed a football broadside into our neighbors' guts. Woom! we
hollered, and cupped our hands like running backs to keep ourselves
from harm.

Woom! Soon there were pledges who moaned. Pledges who doubled up
and wished this half hour gone. Woom! And there were brothers who
joined, standing among the tough guys like Jim Ulsh and Dave Mazur
and Cecil Clifford, the ones who never showed fear or pain.

Woom! We fired back, driving that ball into the stomach of seniors just
returned drunk from bars. Woom! Until Jim Ulsh took that ball point
first and came apart inside. Woom! Until Dave Mazur cracked a rib
because that ball thunked wide.

We were five days into the mandatory week of no sleep. We were nearly
finished with Woom! ball, one more night, and I was left standing beside
Cecil Clifford, who screamed Woom! like a sound could take the air out
of me, neither of us knowing he would die in a war that was as small,
that night, as our skirmish. Woom! I shouted, and nobody stepped
between us until that circle broke for the road where we ran into the

town that was sleeping, watching for lights in windows at quarter to four, guessing whether whoever moved there was coming home from trouble or waking into a day that, starting this early, was pain.

JANUARY 1967: THE IMPOSSIBLE

College down to its final semester,
It was, I vowed, my last winter of walking
In terrible weather. The mornings I slogged
Through snow, I thought I could see myself
In the near future of beating the draft,
Shuffling from the physical with the joy
Of a small, but unacceptable flaw.
In Florida, where I planned to be,
Three astronauts had died on the ground,
Inhaling the toxic smoke of a flash fire,
Their deaths grafting them to my classmate
Crushed by a jeep in basic training,
All the danger of the war months away.

That weekend, stopped by sirens, I learned
A girl who'd just said goodbye to me
Had died in the car she'd chosen thirteen miles
Before, that whatever else she'd meant
To say had been hurled through a windshield.
Like she could have been, I was riding
With Cecil Clifford, who was going
To explode in the air over Vietnam,
But right then, just after 2 a.m., we shared
The expletives that follow sudden death
And added the sentences full of "if,"
The paragraphs stuffed with stories meant as
Consolations for the impossible.

On the news, January shutting down,
Were tributes to Grissom, Chaffee, and White
That were still filled with fault speculations
About frayed wires, oxygen level, the hatch
Too difficult to reach, and I told myself
I wanted to hear what that sophomore,
The driver, had to say about speed and ice
And drinking because even I had known
Enough to rely on the judgment
Of Cecil Clifford the way I relied
On somebody every night when what
I wanted was more than two miles from school,
Riding in five cars a week, half of them
Driven by soldiers-to-be, without
Saying a word about the test flights

We were taking to decide what was worth it,
What was not, turning up the radio
So impossibly loud a siren
Couldn't slow any of us who believed
We were learning quickly enough to live.

PROPHECIES, NOVEMBER 1969
One night a man pulled his stool
Closer to tell me my fortune was
Written on the pages of an old
Life magazine he laid out on the bar.
"As infallible as the Bible,"
He declared. "Choose four pages
Without ads, and I'll learn you
Your job, your wife, your children,
And the city where you'll end up."

And why not, I thought, because
I'd begun reading again, delaying
My life-to-be that appeared, each night,
On the television news. I was waiting
For a pizza, a drink, and the luck
Of the new draft lottery. I wasn't
Pacifist. I wasn't crippled or criminal
Or employed at anything but
Graduate school, willing to pay
Two beers while I loosened
The pages so I could choose,
For once, tomorrow at random.

I heard salesman, Sarah, None
And Cleveland, enough of that,
But he insisted me back
To *Life* to fill my skeptic hand
With the number of the year I'd die.
And what-the-hell, I flipped
To "This one," and watched him drink
And run his fingers slowly down
The Tet-Offensive text until
He smiled and clapped me across
The shoulders, laughing at the lifeline
He'd counted down for me,
The two of us laughing, then,
Like fortunate friends safe in homes
And health, and I didn't believe
Anything that prophet was saying.

MAY 4: LUCK, SKILL
Just often enough somebody comes back

From certain death, enough to make us think
We're the ones who will go on like my friend
Thrown clear of the T-Bird that exploded
On impact, the neighbor's boy who survived
Ten minutes under cold water, even
Myself skidding into a four-wheel drift
Across a low median and both lanes
Of oncoming, rush-hour freeway traffic
Or sliding into the prone position
Across the asphalt of a parking lot
After a volley of gunfire began.
Going unscathed. Going upright again.
Nothing miraculous like surviving
A free fall ten thousand feet to a swamp.
I rejoined the loud, astonished traffic,
Not talking of escape like the pilot
Who'd brought in a plane with a blown hatch door,
Ferrying a full manifest of ghosts
Back to the everyday task of living.

Safely on earth, the one in a thousand,
He spoke about trying to keep that plane
Alive, throttling up, working the small chance
Of improvisation while it banked left
And dove, drawn sideways and down by its wound.
"If I land this thing," he said to laughter,
Was the first phrase of a hurried promise
That ended with "all the rest of my life."
And then he started the full-time labor
Of silence about how, after those first
Minutes of surviving, he knew he would
Never again be so skillful, that it

Saddened him until he seemed an athlete
Just retired, his gratitude so awkward
And false he knew this was the first day of
The long sentence of dissatisfaction.

MOTHER'S DAY, 1970

"They should have shot you, too," my uncle said,
After I chose between the protesters
And the blunt authority of the Guard.
Sick of my muttonchops and thick mustache,
He hated how I thought I knew the world
Better than he did without picking up
A gun or grenade or the requisite
Gumption to wear a uniform with pride.
That Sunday I was back home from Kent State
Where classes had been canceled on account
Of jerks and whiners like me. My father,
The one brother of four who hadn't aimed
And fired at Nazis, sat silently through
That long oral exam for loyalty,
My uncle repeating, "Look at yourself,"
Like a therapist for family,
Waiting while I drifted to France where men
Who had followed him were guessing their odds
Against the higher ground of the Fascists,
Each of those men staring at my uncle
For the terrible, opened lips of "Go."

ALL THROUGH MAY 1970

I hitchhiked, believing in the kingdom
Of rootlessness. I was naming myself
By choices, whether I wanted to be

Wounded or dead or the distance runner
Of regret. I carried a small, silly
Suitcase for personal items, saying
Nothing to bored or curious drivers
About my history of presidents
By name: Kennedy, the office-buyer;
Johnson, the quitter; Nixon, the liar,
Who had called my classmates "bums" and killed them
Three hundred yards from my classroom at Kent.
I was waging the old revolution
Of flight, using the pity of strangers
And all of the name-calling that followed
Whiskey chased by beer. By the beginning
Of June, I rode home to re-up at Heinz,
Earning enough to start my last term of
Listening to the lectures of others.

WHERE THE BACK SEAT HAD BEEN REMOVED

In Ohio, near Youngstown, two hundred miles
Into hitching, I climbed inside a stranger's
Idling car, one ride closer to Pittsburgh,
And this driver promised me as far as
Sharon after he dropped off his cargo.
I might have panicked then, imagining
His claim an excuse for forced seclusion,
But he said, "What do you think's in there?"
Meaning the four steel cans he carried
Where the Ford's back seat had been removed.
Milk, I thought, but didn't guess, satisfied
With "No idea" before he said
"Nitro" as if I'd believe anything.
"It don't abide shaking," he added,

And I told myself *not possible*
As he described how we would vanish
Like the Japs at Hiroshima, neither
Cruel nor clowning, just, as drivers did,
Making conversation to pass some miles.
There were railroad tracks we crossed so slowly
I had time to expect an imminent,
Personal hell, and yet I sat inside
That car while two strangers unloaded,
Repeating this couldn't be the day
For disaster, not when the work looked
As routine as the milkweed and burdock
That bordered the factory's loading dock,
The bare bulb of the sun suspended above
A lot so sparse with cars I believed
Most workers parked elsewhere so something
Of themselves would survive a mistake,
The small promise of the road straight south
To home from Sharon, Pennsylvania,
As trivial as the curses those can loaders
Shouted so much in unison they seemed
To be chanting the stunted chorus
Of a well-known song while I listened
To my muscle and bone and voices
Saying the same things over and over
About the necessity of balance.

FRATERNITY BROTHERS, 1970
Two years, Rich Cook had lived across the hall,
Giving me rides in his damaged car
Where we breathed the stink left behind
By a creek that flash-flooded hood high,

But this summer Cook was a soldier
In the Ohio Guard, and I was
Reading the Victorians and Faulkner
At Kent State where classes had resumed.
Since my second beer, I'd been posturing
As a near-miss survivor, and now
Cook was drunk and angry and ready,
He said, to shoot me if history
Repeated itself. He had a pistol
In that flooded Ford I could see through
The screen door where white moths were frantic
To enter, and he wondered out loud
If I'd piss myself if he decided
To show-and-tell me just how cowardly
I could be up close with him and brother
Bowers just back from two tours and a pair
Of Purple Hearts, somebody who'd survived
Hamburger Hill and nameless night patrols.
Cook asked if I was a Communist now
Or just some big-mouth asshole drinking
His beer with someone who was worth a shit,
And I was ready to renounce my years
Of secondhand graduate essays,
All of those sweet-sounding platitudes
Seeming as simple as pre-meal prayers
While I was composing apologies
And expecting both brothers to lay
A combat-ready beating upon me.
I could say the overhead kitchen light
Beamed a Saint Paul moment of self-knowledge
And conversion, but what it did was
Flicker once when the refrigerator

Hummed into life just before Bowers
Said "Fuck the Guard" so matter-of-factly
I heard the period drop into place,
Ambushing one argument, at least,
In Youngstown where May was fishtailing
Into June, the three of us positioned
As if we were in our late-sixties rooms,
A telephone hanging outside Cook's door,
The black receiver Cook had twice torn loose
And carried into my room after
2 a.m., both times silhouetted
Against the light, spitting, "It's for you."

THE SUMMER AFTER

I wore the company's washed boots.
I jammed my hair inside my hat
And pinned it like the old women
Who were first to arrive at church.

I walked fourteen cooling kettles
And carried long-stemmed spatulas
To scrape a shift's mixed cubes of meat
And vegetables, shake loose the salt.

I worked spaghetti with hot dogs,
Friday, four thirty, the day shift
Backed up at three lights I could see
From the seventh story for soup.

That summer, there were new bosses
Back from the war that wanted me
As soon as I filled my transcript.

They sent me into boxcars where

The split bags of dried beans and flour
Roiled white dust around my face.
My second week, I had to kneel
In ice-watered blood to unclog

A set of drains. For half a shift,
Pairs of men had hoisted frozen
Beef slabs, one hundred pounds per lift,
And they were long sick of wading

Ankle-deep. A fresh veteran
Repeated, "Clear the fucking things,"
Said, "Use your fingers" for the flesh
Half fat that thawed into the shape

And size of a hundred drain holes.
I felt for meat and pulled it free.
My other choice was unscrewing
The drain-lid, thrusting my arms to

The bottleneck built as backup.
On the loading docks, those men smoked
Facing the street. A set of tracks

Split the asphalt. The yellow-bricked
Warehouse rose so close, the sun's shift,
In June, was only ten till two.

LATE AUGUST
At intermission, when smiling families

Flickered into the trees from the edges
Of the huge screen at Ranalli's Drive-In,
I rinsed my mouth with whiskey and hooted
At the teenagers who sipped soft drinks while
Their happy-face snack foods skipped to the stars.
I needed to piss and pay for something
Salty for Faye, who wanted to see what
Happened to Steve McQueen. In the men's room,
The cinderblocks repeated "Suck my dick";
The six light bulbs were yellow, one of them
Overhead when I leaned down to vomit
In the sink, my face jammed beneath the faucet
Until some high school boy in tie-dyed shorts
Looked so long I ripped my knees, right, then left,
Into the middle of his colored crotch.
The boy said "Unhhh" and sat. Outside, Faye stood
In line for popcorn and fries we carried
Past a Plymouth where James Brown was groaning
"Hot Pants" as if he were fondling her hips.
Our speaker was face down in the gravel.
On the screen four hamburgers were dancing
Between two cheerful cups of Coke. I pulled
The damp cord, and the tinny trumpets that
Moved their tiny feet heaved up between us.

AFTER SCHOOL REOPENED
The students who had died
Left me old tests and papers;
They'd cleaned out their rooms
And wanted me to file their work
Graded A through F in stacks.
There's no turning down the dead—

Some mornings, a box of scrawls
Sat outside the door. Finally,
The names were torn off, paragraphs
Missing, leaving me to decide
How they began and ended,
Who wrote each one and why.
On my Kent, Ohio, street
Lived a woman whose garage
Was full of found shoes. "Local,"
She told me, "all of them, so it's
Just a matter of time to match."
She showed me a two-tiered shelf.
"So far," she said, "six pairs,
This last one taking a year
To mate," something to tell
The months-dead plagiarist
Who dared our teacher to prove it:
"Where," he said, "in all the world,
Are you going to look?"

WINTER: THE BARTER SYSTEM
After he hit me, the drunk in the truck
Offered fifty-five dollars and a gun.
He said, "OK now, no need for police."
Though there was a left headlight to replace,
A fender to wrestle back from the tire.
On the highway, at 2 a.m., zero
Settling upon us like snow, I didn't
Negotiate because I thought I was
Getting an investment back with interest.
A month before I'd paid fifty dollars,
Total, for that car with steering problems,

And the truth is, I'd been out drinking, too,
My sober-by-comparison nothing
The police would credit. For five months more
I drove that fifty-dollar car until
It leaked oil so badly I drove it
Into a thick-trunked tree to make it quit.
That gun? I kept it in a dresser drawer
Like something loaded with caps. Before then,
I had fired one .22 in my life,
Hitting dirt three times before surprising
The fluttering edge of a pillowcase
Tacked to a tree stump on my uncle's farm.
Finally, I needed ammunition
To get my barter's worth, and I carried
That pistol to a store to size bullets
To barrel, the clerk turning it over
And over in his hands as if he were
Memorizing the serial number
To match a police report on his desk.
"You shoot this here thing and you fixing to
Fuck yourself up," that salesman said at last,
Showing me the crack, how it ran so straight
I'd seen it as design. "Billy the Kid,"
He said, "be cool," and I inventoried
That specialty store like a thief, counting
Three customers, figuring which of them
Would haul my lame story home, including
How flushed I turned, how quickly I beat it
To that car I'd wreck for good in two weeks.
For miles, I steadied at the speed limit,
Checked my mirrors and turned the radio
To murmur, driving ten minutes to where

I flung that pistol off a bridge, timing
The spaced headlights of witnesses until
I was free, in the dark, to let it go.

THE ANNIVERSARIES

Year after year, in May, I read
The wire service for Kent State news.
The veterans speak sadly, stunned
In the empty spring. Some of them
Remember in front of students
Required to attend assemblies.
Nine of these years it's been raining
When I walk outside, counting down
The minutes in Pennsylvania
Or upstate New York, saying "Now,"
Listening to voices and traffic,
Wind and whatever surfaces
Decided that year's sound of rain.

THE CASUAL SLURS

Early in an evening of remembering death,
I tell my friend that after the Kent State shooting,
After students like me went home and waited out
Our anger, the police came armed to Jackson State
Like a re-creation of the Ohio Guard.
They herded those students, I tell him. They backed them
Against the front wall of a dorm and suffered stones
And bricks until they opened fire as if they'd loved
The headlines from the week before, emulating
The Midwest's faux army, sustaining their gunfire
Thirty seconds with an armory of weapons.

Almost five hundred times, I say, they hit that dorm.
Two dead, twelve wounded, all of them "nigger students"
According to the cop who called in the shooting.
That speaker's nickname was "goon," something history
Can't make up, his casual slurs, on tape, leaching
Into the voiceless future to poison language,
The violent separations that mark our speech
Though we've forgotten their indecipherable
Beginnings, ones like birth and the early years, what
We hear about from the mouths of those who love us,
Their stories working to share the unknowable.

HISTORY BITES

One night, in his room, complaining, my son

Sat to steal his report from the *World Book*,
List the Kent State dates and dead like fractions
To be reduced. "History Bites," it said
On his paper, "choose one, taste, and swallow,"
And I surprised him with slides, his father
The student who'd sampled his fresh mouthful
Of wartime after class. Monday, May 4,
Returned on his wall, and he worked the crowd
For someone familiar from the Dark Age
Of flared pants, long hair, and armies. Though I
Was faculty by now, standing in front
Of students with the rifle of language,
I wanted to show myself on his wall
Like some shadow animal of the hands—
Rabbit of the fingers, the knuckled dog,
Decorative pain of the headstone past.
Look, there I am then, I said, history
Whirring in that projector's fan. My son

Said, "What were you doing?" and I managed
"Watching," followed silence with "I don't know"
As if he were asking why I'd never
Left college or written one word on
History as it happened: Some roar of oaths
Striking the raised oath of rifles; some pop
Of gestures freeing the pop of gunfire—
Like fireworks, one platitude for anger,
And what I told my son was "Write this down:
We thought they were blanks; we stood ignorant
As some lost tribe staring at sticks that smoked."
Which is the way these histories happen,
Somebody saying "Never," "Of course not,"
Or its thousand variants. The crowd scene
That follows, the jostling forward of faith.

85

SEQUEL

The planets of difference seem
Perfectly centered, all of them
Preparing for an invasion.
Now each country walks in the paths
Of righteousness. When the planes fly
Into our cities, my children
And theirs will call for the comfort
That comes from love. We will listen
To each other's voices until
The world we have made together
Splits and scatters like providence.

THE POSSIBILITIES FOR WINGS

How often have the customs of strangers
Silenced me into dreaming their beliefs?

In Java, for example, some people
Insist the souls of suicides return
In the bodies of crows, while in Scotland,
Souls of the lonely flee to butterflies.

In Pennsylvania? In this town where death
Belongs to those with names I've said, the souls
Of the ordinary are cries called out
And gone into an afternoon of rain,
Leaving me to wish winged things for the friend
Whose heart has failed, the friend who killed himself
In his meticulously sealed garage.

In my backyard? I'm talking to the friend
Who, like me, has sidestepped the terrible,
And even, from time to time, laughs aloud,
Neither of us, not yet, fluttering off
In moths or whatever we might predict
For our futures, the possible wings for
Depression, jealousy, the waste of hours.

Choose one? he asks, and I say the poorwill,
The only bird that hibernates, waking,
After months, to flight. Yes, he answers, good.
Overhead, just now, a small plane pierces
The air, and I imagine both of us
Onboard, becoming birds that seem to fly
Without love of anything but ourselves,
Shaping our fear against the summoned sky.

iii.

The Chernobyl Swallows

In April, near the anniversary
Of catastrophe, barn swallows returned,
Flying inside the exclusion zone to
Nest in the radioactive ruins.

Like disciples, the swaddled scientists
Marveled. The work crews, weeks later, toasted
The newly hatched, especially the fledged
With albino feathers after they soared

Like their siblings, devouring insects
With the ravenous hunger of swallows.
For months, the left-behind celebrated
How weak the worst was, and when the swallows,

No exceptions, flew southward, how feeble
Apocalypse could be. But come spring, not
One of the white-flecked birds returned, only
The ordinary nesting and spawning

Their own mutations. Families, by then,
Had moved back to where the world was quiet
And uncrowded, reclaiming rooms inside
The official radius of poison.

And through succeeding springs, no flight with white
Above them, just guards and squatters were left
To praise what they took for heroism,
Even if only among the swallows.

Turning Sixty-Five: How to Rid
Your House of Ghosts

Politely, but firmly, ask them to leave.
Convince each one that the physical world
Is no place to hide from elder spirits
Who will, with time, forgive their trespasses.

Even if the early evening predicts
How the midsummer moon will reflect
Perfectly off the river near where
I've wandered, a calm premonition

The ghosts of the family seem docile,
But those who died young are quick to anger.
They track their war wounds into the kitchen
Like mud, spill accident traumas that stain.

Has surfaced like this birthday,
This section of the Susquehanna,
Shallow in a dry July, leering
At the raised floodplain houses nearby.

They're not to blame for loitering like bums.
Don't you be angry, too. They'll feed on it.
Likewise, don't show fear. Ghosts are animals
Who smell opportunity in weakness.

Wearing bright ties, three white-shirted men,
Brilliant as moons, came to my door
This week, each of them proposing
The gift of financial protection.

No luck? Try smudging. Open the windows
In each room and walk burning sage throughout.

Tell them, "Spirits leave." If you're embarrassed,
Professionals will do this for a fee.

> I sweated through the short workouts
> Of nonchalance, but nothing shut up
> Their prophecies but the promise to work
> Another year, postponing paradise.

You may have outlived some for fifty years,
So they're rightfully sick of your breathing
And the terrible leisure of language,
Sentences transparent as childhood lies.

> A man, yesterday, displayed a badge
> That signaled he was FBI,
> And I sorted my mortal sins as
> He seated himself in my office.

All your uneventful days are enough
To anger anyone. If it wasn't
For knowing that horror is certainty,
They would bury their phantom teeth in you.

> And though he asked about the morals
> And patriotism of a student,
> He might as well have been a specialist
> Holding the proof of a shadowed scan.

Safety is as tenuous as cupping
The groin. What matters, for serenity,
Is believing in your words. When the house
Feels empty, bless it in the name of God.

Since waking, I've heard "however"
In every declarative sentence:
The river can be waded here
By treading the rippling path of moon.

Visiting the Living Writers Class

When a student, guessing my age,
Asked whether I thought my best work
Was behind me, I launched a joke
About shadows and how to face
Away from light, fooling no one,
Least of all that girl who waited
For a decisive yes or no.
Seriously? I asked, the word
Sounding like a Doppler effect
Passing scream. I worried she'd say
I'd finished my three-score and ten,
That every word from now on was
One more reminder of decline.
Even the bored business majors
In the back were leaning forward,
Maybe setting a price upon
My reputation. They'd purchased
A book of mine or shared to save
Money for cheap beer and pizza,
What they were looking forward to
At 9 p.m. when they were free.
Hadn't I begun by joking
I was pleased to still qualify
As a subject? Didn't I say
My "selected poems" might be
A synonym for summary
Before I'd join the huge chorus
Of the dead? The girl beside her
Asked if I had published before
Her mother was born; somebody
Googled my name beside a date
Of birth; the professor noted

She was half my age, everyone
Going so bright with division
That the room turned otherworldly
With the brief flare of history.
The class, attentive at last, loved
Transience, listening, rapt, as
I approached the intersection
Where traffic vanishes, looking
Both ways under fluorescent lights,
And before I began to stand,
They fluttered up their hands, anxious
As patients who wanted to know
What they could do when nothing called.

The Hands

Because, my father said, his hands
looked as if they had never done
a day's work, even in age, smooth
white, and untouched, my great-uncle,
for decades, was a hand model
in magazines and newspapers.

My father's hands were always white
with flour, dusted to roll dough
into spheres, left- and right-handed,
to model forms for sandwich buns
while I relied upon the right,
unable, after seven years
of Friday night work, to master
the art of left-handed circles.

Years before, bare-handed, a man
had pulled a pan of sandwich buns
from the oven without burning
himself. My father, some Fridays,
would tell that story whenever
miracles were mentioned. As if
we needed faith, as if that man
never again forgot his gloves.

A woman born with three fingers
now experiences, after
amputation, a phantom hand
with five fingers. She has become
phenomenon. As if those bones
had needed years of weather to

expose them, an old crime revealed
from a life long before this one.

My mother had a small scrapbook
of clipped ads that featured hands. Here,
she said, are his, and there. Looking
was like taking an IQ test.
Which of these are identical?
Which one of those doesn't belong?

My daughter, an artist, teaches
anatomy to small children,
beginning, each year, with the hands.
Her daughter, at five, drew my hands
like a camera. At seven,
she sketched my face so perfectly
I feared that my secrets would be
revealed through her accomplished hands.

Although rare, there have been cases
of men and women who bite off
fingers from their own hands. Often,
they beg to be restrained. If left
alone, they disfigure themselves.

My mother's uncle lived forty
years beyond modeling, his hands
so unspotted for so long they
seemed to suggest that his body
was unspeakably pink and soft.

Dreamtime

For the Kimberley of Australia, supernatural beings called Wondjina existed in Dreamtime, wandering the earth and shaping the land.

1. ALWAYS, THE SPIRITS BROUGHT WATER;
THEY DRESSED IN RAIN.
The first family subject was work,
the length and value of it, wages
taboo unless they were earned by the dead—

What was made at the end of a day?
Bread and steel, soup and railroad cars, highways
and the immaculate rooms they lived in.

2. THE SEEDS WOULD SPROUT AS HUMAN,
SO THE SPIRITS SOWED THEM.
For thirty-eight years, counting from my birth,
I had eight aunts and uncles by blood,
eight more by marriage, all of them unscathed.

On the left side, front to back, they filled
so many pews, so early, the service
looked like a wedding, a funeral.

3. THE LANDSCAPE WAS ART, SO THE WONDJINA
SHAPED THE EARTH.
In pairs, with children, they moved and scattered,
built with brick and wood in seven states,
in snow, in never-ending warmth, in faith.

All but my parents formed a second life

before they hardened, reshaping themselves
with rivers and oceans, accents, love.

4. FINISHED WITH THEIR WORK, THE SPIRITS
BECAME THE PAST.
None of them had pets, so nothing died but
their parents, decades when the past stayed as
constant as myth. And then, for twenty years,

they vanished, leaving only my father
to dream them as children who promised
they were shaping his eternity.

Elegy

1

In the Los Alamos museum,
topical board games
Up an Atom and *Nuclear War*,
fast-paced and humor
promised for all ages.
Nearby, a photograph
of an Atomic Cake,
tiny models of battleships
floating on blue icing
beside a whipped cream,
rising, mushroom cloud.

2

Twenty feet wide, a space
has opened in the roof
of a Hanford tunnel where
nuclear waste is stored,
robots sent to test and repair,
eight feet of soil
prescribed to prevent
an airborne radiological event
escaping a tunnel
that holds railroad cars
of radioactive waste,
literally, this summer,
seventy years young,
my mother's phrase
for the old, yet active,
an age she did not reach
to verify its truth.

3

In six hatbox-sized cans that once held
syrup-soaked peaches, cherries, or apples
for my father's bakery pies, my mother
saved the photos left behind by the dead,
thousands of formal-occasion poses,
the oldest become strangers,
unidentified by aunts and uncles
who knew those faces so well they never
thought to caption them. For twenty years,
my father kept those cans buried
in his basement like time capsules.
When I opened them, he shook his head
to every face, even my mother's as a child.

4

A confession:
I am in love
with the bottom shelf
of a seldom-used closet
where a picture
of nearly identical
hot peppers lies boxed
in one thousand pieces
beside another
labeled "beyond expert,"
hundreds of swirls
in gold and white
broken into
twelve hundred pieces
so like each other
they have lain scattered

on the dining room table
for nearly a month.

5

In the Los Alamos museum,
a sign read, *After Nagasaki,*
no other bombs were detonated
until the United States set off
two more in July, 1946. "To scare
the shit out of the rest of the world,"
a white-bearded, wheelchaired man
hissed from my left, his breath aided
by a canister of oxygen.

6

Where my father's bakery was located,
there were, in case of fire, address codes
counted by the fire hall's bell.
Butler Street was 3. The bakery 629.
Ten months my father had owned
that business. And I was four when,
one Sunday, that sequence pealed,
nothing for either of us to do but watch
the volunteers do the work of saviors.

7

A student, once, lectured me about
the significance of omens,
finding the end-times revealed
in the behavior of politicians.
He was withdrawing from school
to concentrate on minimizing

what he possessed, including all
the fundamental desires of the body.
He'd add me to his prayers, he said,
confident he could lessen the pain
of my eternal punishment.

8

That old man in the museum
said his science, during the war,
was censored, citing, for example,
the confiscation of his books.
And when, to impress, I said,
"I was born almost to the day
of the first test," he asked,
"Your father an educated man?"
Candid at last, I answered, "No,"
and listened while he hissed,
"Well, he didn't know what he was
getting you in for, most likely."

9

Behind the puzzles, inside a shoebox,
three certificates from a month
of puffed rice, each for a square inch
of land in the Yukon. Underneath,
from a summer of Wheaties,
six miniature, all-metal license plates—
collect all forty-eight—
and nineteen wallet-sized photos
of fourth grade classmates whose names,
without labels, I am able to recite.

10

For twenty years, my father lived
alone, his basement shelves stocked
with necessities bought in bulk
on sale. He wore a medical alert
that read, Do Not Resuscitate.
Whenever I visited, my father,
the not-so-well-educated man,
said he felt sorry for me because
I would live to experience hell-on-earth.

11

During my last semester of teaching,
to clear shelves, I gave away books
to students. They smiled and thanked me,
and each time I recognized
my generosity as a symptom of dying.

12

When, at ninety, my father
surrendered to a senior center,
his room a bed and board games
played with volunteer visitors,
he reversed the status of his alert,
asking to be returned to the living.
What was it that room might have held?
Something striking or unique?
Something impossible to cede?

Anniversary

If half of happiness is genetics,
What consolation there is in knowing
That some bees, now, prefer sex with orchids
That have evolved to irresistible.
Because bitterness ascends each evening
Like the moon. Because the leaves of houseplants
Are dusted with fear as we tend to them.
Because we believed, once, that they adored
Our songs, that they and our unborn children
Were happier hearing those melodies.
Now my student, nineteen, says she's been raped;
Yours, eleven, is pregnant, yet we live
In an envied place. Now epidemics
Of hive death have struck, local beekeepers

Repeating pollution and pesticides,
Proliferation of cell phone towers.
A white whale, nonfiction, has been sighted;
White rain has fallen on New Mexico.
In the museum we visited today,
A history of our sick presidents,
Their doctors and their treatments—pneumonia,
Ileitis, cancer, stroke. And what's more—
Bright's and Addison's disease, depressions,
Their recoveries, deaths, and even so,
We were in Philadelphia, minutes
From the Liberty Bell and the tourists
Who travel here because we've muddled through
The way our early presidents came back
From bleeding a pint or more for fevers.
At last, when we looked at a killer's skull,
When we examined his brain in fluid,
I told you about the Nazi doctors

Who searched the brains of four hundred children
They had murdered to discover their dreams,
And you said "impossible" like a child.
Listen, butterflies and moths remember
Their lives as caterpillars, the hunger
And the constant dream of flight. Honeybees
Can recognize a face. Margaret Bell
Owned bees that flew five miles to mourn her death,
Gathering near her house for an hour.
If, as scientists tell us, most women
Are happier than men until they turn
Sadder at forty-eight, then here, writing now
Past sixty, I must believe my darkness
Is nothing like the midnight you suffer.
Someone, now, has made the blackest substance
Ever known, worse than the blind-dark of caves.
The world's dirt is disappearing faster
Than ever before. "Gary, just you wait,"
My mother promised me ten thousand times,
And I did until this moment, saying
That I've woken, love, to some happiness
All forty years in this bed beside you

Acknowledgments

Individual poems and entire sequences have appeared in:

"The Possibilities for Wings," *Virginia Quarterly Review*
"History Bites," *Beloit Poetry Journal*
"Shadowing the Gravedigger," *The Southern Review*
"The Absolute," *American Literary Review*
"The Fury that Follows Small Disappointments," "The Startling
    Language of Shriveling Leaves," "Distraction Therapy," and
    "The Casual Slurs," *Prairie Schooner*
"Upon the Tongue," *Alaska Quarterly Review*
"The Secret City" and "Elegy," *American Journal of Poetry*
"After the Bomb Drill, Miss Hartung Teaches Weather," *Green
    Mountains Review*
"For Good," *Hampden-Sydney Poetry Review*
"Preserving Cursive" and "Worship," *Seminary Ridge Review*
"The Lost Continents," "The Impossible," "May 4: Luck, Skill," and
    "The Fear Warehouse," *The Literary Review*
"The Sum Total," *Southern Poetry Review*
"The Chernobyl Swallows," *The Somerville Times*
"The Perimeter Melody," *Roger*
"The Secret Voice," *Poet Lore*
"The Rain after Sunrise," *Willow Springs*
"Stunned," *North American Review*
"The Shelter Revival," *Free State Review*
"The Malignancy of Stars" and "Assessing the Dead," *Valparaiso Poetry
    Review*
"Science," *I-70 Review*
"The Infinity Room," *Lake Effect*

"Merging, Slowing, the Second Sun" and "Anniversary," *Paterson
    Literary Review*
"During the Retirement Semester," *The Gettysburg Review*
"Woom! Ball," *The Alembic*
"Late August," *Poetry Northwest*
"Winter: The Barter System," *Pleiades*
"The Lengthening Radius for Hate," in a much shorter version, was
    published as a chapbook by Cervena Barva Press.
"May 4: Luck, Skill," "Mother's Day, 1970," "All through May 1970,"
    and "The Anniversaries" were published in different form as
    "The Shooting" in *Zone 3*.
"Upon the Tongue" was reprinted on Poetry Daily.
"The Lost Continents" was reprinted as part of a WebDelSol online
    chapbook.

WHEELBARROW BOOKS

Anita Skeen, *Series Editor*

Sarah Bagby	Carolyn Forché
Mark Doty	Thomas Lynch
George Ellenbogen	Naomi Shihab Nye

Wheelbarrow Books, established in 2016, is an imprint of the RCAH Center for Poetry at Michigan State University, published and distributed by MSU Press. The biannual Wheelbarrow Books Poetry Prize is awarded every year to one emerging poet who has not yet published a first book and to one established poet.

SERIES EDITOR: Anita Skeen, professor in the Residential College in the Arts and Humanities (RCAH) at Michigan State University, founder and past director of the RCAH Center for Poetry, director of the Creative Arts Festival at Ghost Ranch, and director of the Fall Writing Festival

The RCAH Center for Poetry opened in the fall of 2007 to encourage the reading, writing, and discussion of poetry and to create an awareness of the place and power of poetry in our everyday lives. We think about this in a number of ways, including through readings, performances, community outreach, and workshops. We believe that poetry is and should be fun, accessible, and meaningful. We are building a poetry community in the Greater Lansing area and beyond. Our undertaking of the Wheelbarrow Books Poetry Series is one of the gestures we make to aid in connecting good writers and eager readers beyond our regional boundaries. Information about the RCAH Center for Poetry at MSU can be found at http://poetry.rcah.msu.edu and also at *https://centerforpoetry.wordpress.com* and on Facebook and Twitter (@CenterForPoetry).

The mission of the Residential College in the Arts and Humanities at Michigan State University is to weave together the passion, imagination, humor, and candor of the arts and humanities to promote individual well-being and the common good. Students, faculty, and community partners in the arts and humanities have the power to focus critical attention on the public issues we face and the opportunities we have to resolve them. The arts and humanities not only give us the pleasure of living in the moment but also the wisdom to make sound judgments and good choices.

The mission, then, is to see things as they are, to hear things as others may, to tell these stories as they should be told, and to contribute to the making of a better world. The Residential College in the Arts and Humanities is built on four cornerstones: world history, art and culture, ethics, and engaged learning. Together they define an open-minded public space within which students, faculty, staff, and community partners can explore today's common problems and create shared moral visions of the future. Discover more about the Residential College in the Arts and Humanities at Michigan State at *http://rcah.msu.edu.*